# Peaks and Valleys:

## A Traveler's Guide

Getting Closer to God
Harnessing Power of Mind
Innerstanding Consciousness
Managing Relationships
Synchronistic Awareness
Protecting Life Force
The Material Plane

Joseph Louis

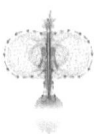

Æthereal Material

**Peaks and Valleys:**
A Traveler's Guide

By Joseph Louis

ISBN:          978-1-966313-01-4


Email: joesall.js@gmail.com


Please visit patreon.com/etherealmaterial to contact the author directly about PDF purchase. Ebook and audiobook available online.


Youtube:
https://www.youtube.com/@joesalvador
https://www.youtube.com/@JoeSalvador-production


A special thanks to all the contributors supporting this endeavor to carefully organize and compile a collection of notes, references and applications in a series digestible to the reader and resourceful to the spirit and the mind.

*This book is dedicated to my mother, father, and sister. Thank you for your continued support over the years. You are deeply appreciated on levels transcending words. With Love,*

*- Joe*

# CONTENTS

Introduction............................................................5

1) Getting Closer to God...............................................7

2) Harnessing Power of Mind...............................21

3) Expressing Consciousness...............................31

4) Managing Relationships...................................39

5) Synchronistic Awareness...................................45

6) Protecting Life Force.........................................52

7) The Material Plane.............................................57

# INTRODUCTION

Presenting to the student of Life *University* tremendous

opportunities to gain insight and wisdom is not a light or

easy task. Myself a student, I remember I am here as a

messenger, or transmuter, of energies, vibrations, and

frequencies emanating from Source. The infinite potential

that surges within, is the same infinite potential without.

That is to reference the popularized phrase, "As above, So

below" or "As within, So without" and its demonstrations

of Power.

From the symbolical references subliminally embedded

into the mainstream *media* (note greek goddess, *Medea;*

meaning *planner*, *schemer*) of entertainment, to the

celestial luminaries harnessing cymatic fields, or

vibrational phenomena affecting both Mother Earth and

the internal biological systems of all living organisms and

electromagnetic bio-fields within; this collection of notes is

intended to integrate a deeper inner awareness of the

Creative Universe within oneself, irrespective of the common driving narratives that have been interwoven into the matrix and collective mind of humans as powerful, controlling, and manipulative current day belief systems. **Peaks and Valleys** is designed to honorably convey to the reader an innerstanding of *Prana*, or Life Force energy, how it can be manipulated, how to protect Life Force, Power of Mind and effective transmutation of E-motion (energy in motion), the dualistic and non-dualist remedies of the Inner Eye Intuition, polarization of thought in the Lower Planes and it's relations with electricity and magnetism in the Universe. Furthermore, discovering the layers of oneself and how to balance powerful Inner Energy Fields well known as Chakras, Light and Darkness (the Internal Blueprint of Imagination), the Spirit and its perpetual self-contemplation with its relations to the Creative Process, subconscious and consciousness awareness development of Universal synchronicities, and more......

6

## CHAPTER ONE

## PART ONE: GETTING CLOSER TO GOD

Prior to the first breath of a human, the fetus does not need oxygen from inflating lungs due to the placenta providing oxygenated blood through the umbilical cord. Communications exist between the biological systems present and are functioning long before conception commences, and a GOD Intelligence force exists omnipotently in the ALL, the original Womb, Mother Gaia, Matrix. As this omnipresent Life Force exists in the Matrix, we acknowledge its Divine essence and Intelligence capacities in the womb of the child-bearing woman, and in the Breath of all Life of all organisms on Earth.

Mother Earth herself is *breathing*, as she has been for much longer than I or anybody reading this book. An electromagnetic field active and busy relaying frequencies to other celestial bodies, seemingly in communication with one another through mediums of cymatic and photonic transmittance and correspondence back to Earth, and every Receiver attuned to these powerful energy bodies, near unfathomable lengths from one another.

The consciousness field of the human is operating in the electromagnetic spectrum also, as we exist within the Universal constructs of the Matrix. The human consciousness, being a participant and recipient to these electromagnetic waveforms, has the ability to transcend what our common five sensory receptor stimulus signals to the brain and Central nervous system in the lower sensuous realms. We have been intricately interwoven with existence to BE ONE with the ALL, carefully designed with infinite potential of the imagination and unique creative faculties, giving us a responsibility to infinitely expand consciousness as we traverse reality inside this physical vessel or 'avatar' with a multidimensional experience.

As aforementioned, we are traversing through waveforms across a vast electromagnetic spectrum, of which our physical bodies are capable of rendering an extremely limited percentage; the sensory capacity being limited to experiencing what studies show to be less than 1% of universal waveforms interweaving inside the Firmament. Well, let us go back to the term *Responsibility,* or **the ability to respond**. *Respond to what? God. Intuition. Emotions. Gut. Instinct. Spirit. Prana. Potential. Mind. Feelings. Heart.* These frequencies are all parts of the same Divine machinations, as the different anatomical systems inside of the human body have specialized *Spirit Intelligence* guiding harmonious operations; *the* universal band director and conductor.

Yes, we have the divine potential to respond to this omnipresent Life Force Intelligence, *and* we have the Inner awareness to bring forth Light to the darkest corners of our internal Being, unraveling the Spirit as it transcends to its Soul purpose here in its period of self-contemplation (life experience), *and* beyond in its period of transcendence.

## PART TWO: GETTING CLOSER TO GOD-PRACTICAL APPLICATION OF GNOSIS

In *response* to the Light of the Life Spirit that shines through the Darkness, *your* truth must be aligned and balanced internally by you. All of our energy patterns are our responsibility! For whom is supposed to be in charge of such thought habit forms other than the individual? We are here to help each other remember we are never alone, but rather ALL-ONE; that we are self-sovereign Beings who are not in need of government (govern; to control, and Menté, or ment; mind). You are your own leader, and always will be.

Human consciousness has capability of harnessing through listening to the Divine that is inside of You. The Spirit will do whatever it can to stay alive when in a state of Clarity. When one is at peace, listening not with the ears, but Living from the heart, connecting to the heavenly serenade of the cosmic strings emanating the firmament and the eternal realms of the Oversoul.

The ALL-present, Universal Power is electromagnetically transmitting Prana, or Life Force, through *highly advanced* biological systems. Breath intakes oxygen, which chemically activates the blood in the body to move through a complex veinous and arterial system connecting all functioning of the systems together. Now, what part of this do you have to worry about on a daily basis...? For most, humans are generally not thinking about breathing, we just breathe... similar to the heartbeat. We don't generally think about the magnetic vortex of energy that is propelling a mechanical power producing constant electrical output, with an EM field that has been noted to be many, many times greater than that of the brain (anywhere from 100-5000x stronger magnetically, and 100,000x stronger electrically) and can be energetically detected in part of what is known as an *aura,* or *toroidal* vibrational field surrounding a human body not seen with the naked eye. *Kirlian* photography has presented energy fields existing and *flowing* internally and externally in living tissues of plants, animals, and humans. Cymatic arrangements (sometimes with telescopic assistance) of ancient, long known luminary bodies we call planets dance in a theatrical chronology for billions of years. All this to say, these frequencies that are neither created nor destroyed are in a field of Infinite Potential, constantly rearranging and reorganizing when a certain vibration or frequency field begins molding Creative Potential into order in the Material Plane (Spirit into Matter; Chaos into Order) and taken form as physical manifestations in the Creation Field. The combination of Spirit and Matter IS YOU, astral traveler. The boundless potential to BE, is WITHIN. Getting

Closer to God, that is to say, to BE *honorable* with your actions. The essence of ALL exists as an endless flow of potential energies (possibilities) constantly coursing through the Breath of Divine Spirit, in synchronous mechanical and spiritual operations (self-contemplation), much of which is still beyond our full comprehension.

Part Three will further discuss practical application one can utilize in the Matrix to go WITHIN, and unravel the PASSION (passio; to suffer, pain) which is the opposite equivalent of PLEASURE. Meaning, non-dualistically speaking, pleasure and pain ARE the same coin. It is ONE experience to the Universal Mind and to the Spirit. For powerful reference, let us refer back to the first paragraph of the mother bearing the child. One can acknowledge the Pain that IS the experience *with* Joy, Pleasure and Love that fills every inch of the mother after birthing her newborn into the Gaia, our womb, Mother Earth.

## PART THREE: GETTING CLOSER TO GOD- PRACTICAL APPLICATION IN THE HUMAN EXPERIENCE:

Life has no purpose; the purpose is Life. What is possible in the human experience? Harnessing the ability to protect and control Prana, utilizing Mind and enabling flow states of creative purpose in the Mind to cultivate boundlessly in the faculties of the imagination. Yes, a sovereign king or queen you are, as your Intuition is GOD.

The relationships you have with *everything* IS your life experience. *As within, so without.* Who do you listen to? Does most of your life experience consist of consumption, that is, to the external world? Do you spend any time practicing meditation, or in other words, quieting the external world and directing intentions to the internal world? As the spirit perpetually contemplates self, have you given time to listen to it?

Surprisingly, to those who have not traveled the multiple dimensional planes of their collective existence with ALL that is, one will soon acknowledge it does not require special abilities, as the Divine in all humans are *collectively* of a Divine Intelligence Force that is our responsibility to protect and develop *individually,* and together bring human consciousness *collectively* to deeper Awareness.

That is with ALL people, with thoughts, with your habits, with your actions, with Nature, with inanimate objects, with technology, with the plants, the animals, with your *dreams*, the breath you are taking *this moment*, with memories, with your silent whispers and words aloud, with *ALL* that you consume, with your emotions, with the MIND, with GOD. Your relationships *are everything*.

Now, here are some words to take into consideration when developing strategies to optimize healthy energy patterns, eliminating unwanted energy patterns that serve no purpose, transmuting energy patterns that are resourceful BUT are currently being misdirected, and internally tap the reservoir of Prana effectively. Please take your time in this section to study carefully and review the notes as many times as necessary.

– Integrate a **reductionist** mentality when implementing *Soul*ution to the energy patterns that are being focused on. That is, do not over-complicate or overthink, do not *add* multiple supplements to your routine, do not expend your Prana to anything *out of your control.*

– *Separate* from external stimuli serving no higher purpose; eliminate consumption of processed foods, reduce entertainment through digital mediums to a *minimum.* The goal is to redirect the intention of Will, of

Prana, to a healthy mode of *production*. We must practice a deeper connection with our internal Being, our Life Spirit, constantly in a state of self-contemplation.

– Now that we have respectfully quieted the external stimuli, the individual can practice attuning the senses to the internal universe. The *Spirit*. GOD. ALL. Integration of this practice will strengthen the mental and astral planes, as the overstimulation which is now taken away is not negatively affecting vibrational patterning of the thought waveforms in the mind of the individual, allowing *balance* (opposite of balance; *dis-ease)*.

– I would like to make a special note here to suggest to the reader something to remember. That is, one does not have to be in complete silence to access communication with the Inner planes, realms, dimensions; this harnessing Power is Within and certainly available as long as the individual is in commune with the internal Life Spirit. It is also important to note, a key word is *balance,* as one can be subconsciously (unknowingly) manipulated and disrupted by controlled radio, light, sound and other EM frequencies in their environment.

– Once practiced and comfortable, the individual can better *innerstand* the illusive powers of distraction, and the utility of harnessing higher thought frequencies and cultivating faculties of their own inner creative god essence. At this time, we will reflect as much as necessary the *Relationships* with ALL that we do, which *is* the life experience.

– It cannot be explained enough the importance of this section. Please give direct intention to your feelings and emotions, as deeply as necessary, and BE ONE with ALL that is. Certainly, this can be a stopping point for some, as it can lead to discomfort. However, I strongly suggest you stick with the course, and without force, allow yourself to *FEEL*.

– This full embrace with oneself enables amplification of electromagnetic communications with the *Chakras* system, including the **heart**, which we will dive into further detail later on. The flow of *chi, or qi, Prana,* Life Force, can now begin to be redirected at the agency of the individual. We will study these miraculous systems and how to take control of the *currents* of our thought waveforms and biological systems. This section will provide detailed information to reprogram the subconscious mind. The *energy patterns* of habits that are keeping the individual in lower vibrational states of Being (thought and emotion) can and *must be broken* to allow one to harness the sacred fire, the godhead energy inside of us all (the Life Spirit).

   – Furthermore, please note that the creative process of the individual in its purest and immaterial form, is *ever-present* in the perpetual self-contemplation of the Life Spirit. That is the Sacred fire, the soul fragmented and fractal of the omniscient Oversoul, of which each and every vibrational waveform of existence, is inextricably interwoven with one another. GOD. The ALL.

We have reviewed some important notes to consider as we step from the outer edges of the forest and begin traversing deeper wilderness. This course is *not* designed to change your mind. It is designed *for You* to harness Power of Mind and traverse the highest planes of thought and astral planes of potential energies at your WILL, and explore the perpetual Creative Process of the Spirit. The next chapter, *Harnessing Power of the Mind*, will bring to attention the importance of perception, how to neutralize and balance perception, and innerstand non-polarization in Spirit and Mind. The inner world is but a direct reflection of the outer world. *As above, so below.*

# CHAPTER TWO

## PART ONE: HARNESSING POWER OF MIND

Heaven is in the Mind within You, astral traveler. Love is heaven. Love is Light. Light is borne from the Darkness. The continuous cycle exists every day and night, interweaving what appears to be on the external planes. We look up at the sky and observe as the ocean blue ceiling that seems to encapsulate our existence, fades to black, and opens a ceiling of flickering luminaries millions of miles distant.

Humans are ONE with this outer world projection, as all constellations and celestial bodies are moving through internal energy systems of ALL forms of living and non-living, æthereal and material realms. For the human, we contact *internal* Darkness directly when we shut our eyes from Light of the external world. This is an excellent time to pause for a moment, and *read again* the last sentence; for this vital note is acknowledgment of the life experience of human Beings *entering* Internal Darkness *every single day and night cycle*. Our interactions in the Darkness are so common we overlook the fact it happens every day of our waking lives, as we dream and traverse astral realms both during restful periods and waking periods. Is Darkness a portal? Now, back to the stars above.

Astrological mapping was conducted for thousands of years by humans to develop a deeper innerstanding of the Universe.

Whilst mapping these vibrational fields of moving luminaries, sometimes miraculous, spontaneous light shows, atmospheric depressurization and molecular discharges have been recorded as past phenomena throughout centuries. The zodiac is but a mapping of internal vibrational fields of human consciousness for us to resource in its highest frequency forms.

Many *mythologies* were designed to archetypically represent what appeared to be omniscient energy forms that were displayed not only in the heavens, but also in the surrounding environmental bio-fields of electricity and magnetism in the Material plane. For some, this seemed to be *magic of the Gods*! Unexplained phenomena striking *emotions of fear* into the subconscious of many. For other individuals, a deeper curiosity and intention led to profound discoveries seemingly *far ahead* of their time.

This is noted to bring forth the *unraveling* of mythologies to etch into the Universal Collective Mind a *rendition* of their own belief systems, including branching developments of *philosophies and religions*.

Regarding the last two paragraphs, these systems have been interwoven into the Collective Mind and have become undeniably and eternally linked to human consciousness, into the Subconscious Mind of ALL that is. Similarly, 'belief systems' can increase the Power of their existence by harnessing thought frequencies of populations of individuals with limited "like-minded" ideals and *programming* their systems of belief.

Part Two of *Harnessing Power of Mind* will explore the programming constructs inside of the Matrix, how belief systems shape human consciousness, how to develop personal internal belief systems, and utilize the Power of the subconscious mind effectively. At this time, please reference the **Relationships** notes in the previous chapter.

This will carry forward into assuming *responsibility* for the energy patterns we are expressing, transmuting, and redirecting, along with developing awareness for *pattern breaks* in vibrational redundancies that are causing tension, stagnation and imbalance in the electromagnetic bio-field of the individual.

## PART TWO: HARNESSING POWER OF MIND-SUBCONSCIOUS PROGRAMMING, THE INTERNAL SUN AND MOON (THE SOUL AND THE MIND, RESPECTIVELY)

Body, Mind, and Soul = *Earth, Moon,* and *Sun.*
*As Above, So Below. As Within, So Without.*

The human Being is manifesting reality from the inside-out. The individual who *wills* to assume responsibility of the Mind Power and its faculties, recognizes the direct reflection of Mind to Matter, or Material Plane. Most of the human mind is recognized in psychology as the Subconscious, a collective storehouse of everything that has existed in the life experiences of an individual. A storehouse capable of compartmentalizing *every vibrational impression* it receives, and that is absolutely accessible to the individual attuned with the Inner realms.

The Spirit nor the subconscious mind are influenced by polarities in the Material plane. In other words, it does not distinguish between "you" or "I" but rather exists in the higher vibrational fields of the Universal *Chakras* system as Divine Collective Intelligence Life Force.

This is a great time to pause on this note, innerstanding that the programs in the Matrix are heavily influencing both the individual and collective consciousness of humans.

This is not to suggest to the student that anything is particularly good or bad. Again, the non-dualist Mind of the ALL exists with non-polarity. In lower vibrational fields in which we commonly refer to as *Matter,* polarity parameters of thought frequencies can interrupt the natural divine flow of the Life Spirit. A stagnation in energy, especially in the Chakra fields, can arise when polarized thought or habit patterns develop without Inner awareness of transmutative capabilities. The chakra centers experiencing the Material Plane include vibrational fields such as Power, Food, and Sex.

The lower material planes enable the much smaller portion of our consciousness, the conscious mind, to transmit vibratory signals stemming from an incredibly powerful Central Nervous System, that is "plugged in" to constructs inside of the Matrix seeking pleasure and gratification. This, dear students of GOD, is a huge note to remember;

The human experience in the Material Plane IS the purpose and responsibility of the Soul journey in the physical *vessel*, or *avatar*. The two eyes that perceive Light on the external planes must not be the primary source of LIGHT one consumes. The Light from within, born from the Darkness (Imagination blueprint and Subconscious Mind) is the eternal Source and sacred fire that the external world is distracting the student of God from deeply convening.

This brings the reader to furthermore strengthen the objective of these notes, which includes practical application and expansion in the life experience.

## PART THREE: HARNESSING POWER OF MIND- BREAKING THE PATTERN LOOPS, CLOSING THOUGHTS

As we approach the end of Chapter Two, the individual has now been given access to innerstanding how to reprogram their energy patterns and *relationships* existing in their life experience. To review, please see notes (pp. 17-20). Please effectively experiment with exchanging one unhealthy habit (*negative* energy pattern) with another healthy, productive habit (*positive* energy pattern). If you can choose two, then do that alternatively. At the very least, applying some or all of these methods will expand your consciousness and assist in the redevelopment and transmutation of patterns in the individual's *relationships,* both on the inner and external planes (thoughts and actions). This will also develop deeper commune with the Creative Process within the Individual, which is.... You got it! *SPIRIT. LIFE FORCE. PRANA. GOD. ALL.*

Before the student continues to Chapter Three, *Expressing Consciousness,* please consider review and reference of previous chapters as one continues to dive in the following notes, as much as necessary. A focus of this material is to honorably present utilities the student can resource internally, and be ONE with the Mind and ALL that is. A gentle reminder that this book is not here to *change* your Mind. This is for the Spirit on the expansion of truth along the life journey in this Matrix, unraveling an inward adventure of many **Peaks & Valleys,** expressed on multidimensional fields of existence. You are ONE with ALL, astral traveler.

Now, let us advance into the *expressions* of consciousness, a compilation of personal notes important enough to my heart and spirit to dedicate an entire chapter to the subject matter.

# CHAPTER THREE

## PART ONE: EXPRESSING CONSCIOUSNESS

For the purpose of this chapter, the reader will be suggested to allow imagination to ponder the way human Beings are coded *expressions* of Soul and mind, essence of God consciousness, Material Body, and *Spirit*. The Chakra center of the throat is a powerful *expression of consciousness* physically manifested from the higher spiritual centers in the human being and transmitted through vibrations of the vocal cords connected to what one may refer to as the voice box, or larynx. Vibrations create sound waveforms as air passes through them, with which the powerful human instrument of voice becomes exercised into the Material Plane.

This is briefly noted for tangibility and practicality, as the *magic* essence behind the eternal energy flow to this Chakra center is interwoven with soul and subconscious. All of what humans communicate come from some form of consciousness, mostly the collective storehouse of the subconscious mind. As aforementioned, this life experience exists inside of a Matrix system, a construct comprising of an immensely vast spectrum of intricately woven patterns of frequencies and vibrational waveforms. The individual is exactly this, in the form of Divine technology, intertwined of both Spirit and Matter, as ONE Consciousness with ALL that is.

Now, shifting consciousness to the *heart* is where we are directing focus. This is imperative for allowing energy flow through the throat Chakra center and connecting directly with the heart.

This will allow the voice to originate from the *purest* and strongest electromagnetic area of the human body.

This can be accessed through methods introduced in chapter one, *Getting Closer to God*, which is advised to be reviewed again and again for guidance in application of the material as one continues to expand. A goal of innerstanding the subject of *expressions* is to BE the best YOU through mediums of Creative Potential embedded in your *unique* coding, ready to be unraveled from the inner realms of Mind and integrated into building and expanding perception. As the Spirit contained in the vessel continues to self-contemplate, the *response ability* of the individual focuses intention inward, silencing the external, to awaken and convene these powerful, creative inner potential energies. Prana, or Life Force, is now the medium of which the student who has developed a proper attuning to their unique coding can interface and manifest through *expressions* as a divine Life Spirit inside of a technologically advanced program (physical vessel; human body, mother earth).

## PART TWO: EXPRESSING CONSCIOUSNESS- EMOTION = ENERGY IN MOTION

When human emotions are unable to be correctly processed, energy blockages begin to form in the thought activities of the individual, as well as tension, or misdirected energy in the body, causing imbalance, or *dis-ease*. This disruption of Prana is commonly known as *stress*, specifically emotional stress, leading to ailments and lower vibratory states for cancer bodies to potentially invade and replicate *uncontrollably*.

One can easily note how vitally important innerstanding our emotions can be, and how these vibrational states of *feelings* trigger internal response systems in the primal coding of the individual.

If the emotional energies have become disrupted, possessive forces latch themselves to the lower vibrational thought forms associated with *uncontrolled* feelings.

34

These forces are the demiurge existing in the Matrix, negatively affecting the electromagnetic bio-field of the human, possessing the Spirit, and capable of causing extreme vibrational imbalances, addictions, overindulgence, parasitic sickness, and *dis-ease* for extended periods of time.

Developing protection of Prana, creative thought force, and proper emotional expression techniques will encourage the voice to emanate from the heart Chakra, LOVE, and raise the (thought and emotion) frequency fields of the individual for deeper *insight* (the Light of the spirit carries the sacred flame through the Darkness of the subconscious). *IN-SIGHT* or *inner sight* (Inner Eye, Intuition, God) *IS* the Light of the Divine Spirit, born from the Blueprint of Darkness, where imagination and visualization are *vital tools* in the powerhouse of the Mind for the individual to harness and utilize in the Matrix construct.

Having the ability to critically *exercise* and cultivate in the Mind and Imagination without disruption or distraction is one of the most notable and incredible technology features of the synchronous miracles in human anatomy and physiology, and the psychological capabilities one may harness and develop with an *inner* awareness and *willful* intent.

## PART THREE: EXPRESSING CONSCIOUSNESS-HEALING THY SELF, CLOSING THOUGHTS

True healing is built in to the human nature, and always will be. The Mind heals the body, as this Life Force Intelligence some call by the name of God is perpetually *alive* in vibrational *expressions,* permeating the Firmament, mother Earth, what many today call *sun* and *moon,* as well as the other celestial luminaries. This GOD Intelligence permeates *ALL* that is.

The *Real* world, or *reality,* for the individual is constructed *Within* mental states of *realization,* thought frequencies and imagination fields. This is crucial to note, astral traveler, for the external world is but an array of photons (electromagnetic Light frequencies from the *sun,* eternally flowing and arranging in this Gaia Matrix waveforms field) across a spectrum with which humans have been "plugged in" by the brain and spinal cord, or central nervous system. This external world sensorially limits the individual to a physical perspective, as the Material Plane transmits stimuli via the five senses, with all five of them directly jacked into the coding of a simulacrum. The outer world is but a picture *reflecting* the inner world. As within, So without. Extended notes referring to the Material Plane will be presented in the final chapter of **Peaks and Valleys.**

With that addressed, we will transition into Chapter Four, *Managing Relationships,* to assess the importance of innerstanding how to utilize the **Heart** Chakra, harnessing the Prana reservoirs of boundless capacity to Love, and in depth perspectives of practical applications for the *magus* to integrate into their energy patterns (thoughts and actions), if desired. Yes, astral traveler, you are the *Alchemist.*

# CHAPTER FOUR

## PART ONE: MANAGING RELATIONSHIPS-
## HEART CHAKRA, A BALANCING CENTER

We have noted the importance of the higher energy vortices in the upper Chakras systems, the connections to one another in the realms, and perpetual flow of higher frequencies flow from Source into Creation.

This chapter, regarding the **Heart** chakra, will describe this *vital* energy center in the human EM bio-field as the *balancing center* for the upper and lower planes, or dimensions, in the human consciousness and life experience.

Please consider reviewing any personal notes one has recorded up to this point, and reference earlier chapters for a mind refreshment. The paragraph below will greatly assist with this, from *Chapter One: Part Three:*

*"That is with ALL people, with thoughts, with your habits, with your actions, with Nature, with inanimate objects, with technology, with the plants, the animals, with your dreams, the breath you are taking right now, with memories, with your silent whispers and words aloud, with all that you consume, with your emotions, with the MIND, with GOD. Your relationships are everything."*

Now, getting right to the point.... the *balance point* that is. When individuals become consumers in modern day first-world environments, with accessibility to all the conveniences, choices, freedoms and services that exist, the systems of consumption begins to *flood* the natural biological human systems, stagnating the flow of human consciousness, and redirecting the flow of energies in the bio-field (Chakras) to an imbalanced *pattern looping* in the lower Material Planes, or *hell*.

Pause here. This is a critical note, and coming next, is a key to unlocking the Heart Chakra, the *equilibrium point* for the seven Chakras system. Relationships in the lower, material self are *ensnared* by the physical nature of the self, the *ego,* transmitting emotions and actions into lower energy patterns such as greed, impatience, gluttony, addiction, lust, overindulgence, envy, etc..

The word *heaven* reflects balance in the mind, the spiritual higher self of the individual, manifested inside the body, harmonizing *both* spiritual and material aspects of our Being, and living from the *heart,* or *equilibrium.*

## PART TWO: MANAGING RELATIONSHIPS-REDUCTIONIST METHOD

At this time, please review the *reductionist* method on pages 17-21. Everything we experience is based on a relationship we have with some *body* or some *thing.* Advancements in nano and bio-technology continues to intensify, and the reliance and dependency on technological 'services' are merging with the collective consciousness of human life. This, dear friends, is no GOD for you or I to depend or rely on for *anything.*

To clarify, this is not to discourage one from the *utilization* of technological advancements for healthy and benevolent purposes for self and others.

Nor is this to say any particular thing is GOOD or EVIL.

It IS BOTH. And ALL is ONE; inside of you and I, too.

This is to rather encourage the individual to *let go* of the energy patterns that are stagnating the Life Spirit. Potential energy will begin to *FLOW* powerfully in the body when the individual rids overconsumption, and the capability of transmutation grows internally. With *inner* consciousness *expanding,* reaching what some refer to as *christ consciousness;* living in harmony with Intuition, embracing love, and being *honorable* with your actions.

This will conclude the first learning section of **Peaks and Valleys.** I hope you have found Insight with some of this material. This is only to be a utility in the tool belt of your consciousness.

YOU are responsible for awakening the dormant thought forms inside of your *youniversity (inner-verse)*, developing and refining these techniques along the life journey to be *useful*. This material may be used as a stepping stone again and again, until reference is no longer required, and full benefit has been attained by the Spirit of the reader. But that is it, and let it be used for nothing more; we are here to help each other remember, we are ALL ONE. Source. The Infinite Creative Potential surges through your Being. Tap In.

CHAPTER FIVE

**PART ONE: SYNCHRONISTIC AWARENESS**

Every moment is an opportunity to learn, listen, and refine the processes with which one has formed *all relationships through.* If the student has already began to notice patterns in their life experience, in their codes of reality, this synchronistic awareness has already been activated within the consciousness of the individual.

It is an incredibly powerful building tool for the Mind, once initiated into perception, can be consciously brought into *recognition,* or acknowledgement at any moment in time to assist with clarity in decision making and critical thinking.

Another way to express this power is pattern recognition. Humans have an exceptional ability to develop awareness for patterns, as creatures of habit and imitation. However, the levels of repetition and persistence in developing energy patterns can be dangerous without proper guidance, and conscious awareness of practicing a habit is magnetizing the emotion (energy in motion) whether the individual is consciously competent of this or not.

Take note, internal awareness IS the KEY to personal pattern development and synchronistic awareness.

This can be noticed on the external planes of course; but first, this perception is held in the Eye of the Mind, and manifested into physical world as reflected and refracted light frequencies shaping human perspective (optically) through the two eyes on either side of the middle Eye; the sixth Chakra center, the Pineal gland.

It has been traditionally referred to as the Third Eye, however, I personally would suggest replacing it as the First Eye for practical application regarding this subject matter.

## PART TWO: SYNCHRONISTIC AWARENESS-
## FOUR SEASONS INTERNAL CLOCK, THE INNER ZODIAC

All of the seasons are moving through the consciousness of man, perpetually reflections of the Soul and Body. As are the zodiac maps in the sky moving eternally through our entire Being, as well as the elements of æther (**Fire** represents Spirit; **Air** represents Mind; **Water** represents Emotion; **Earth** represents Body). Speaking of synchronicities....

The student has traversed into deep wilderness, and so far successfully developed tools for innerstanding how all that is happening in the outer world, is but a mere reflection of the inner world. Patterns of personal relationships have now reflected themselves in the patterns of the seasons, the constellations, in the Chakras system, and in the awareness of the Spirit. The student is aware that creative potential is boundless and cannot be measured; likewise to the incalculability of the capacity of Mind and ALL that is WITHIN, is ALL that is WITHOUT.

At this point, let us briefly note the symbolical references that dominate the pockets of the modern world around you. These energy patterns should give an idea of who and what is corrupting and trapping the consciousness in lower vibrational fields on Mother Earth with *black magic* rituals.

Or, in other words, *collective, premeditative, malevolent thought patterns expressing through specific shapes and symbols* intended to transmit or *impress* into the subconscious mind of the individuals subject to these vibrational stimuli when introduced into their environment (*potentially* on strategic and carefully planned schedules). I do believe most students who have given intention of expanding their truth have taken notice to this, and what we reference as 'demonic' or 'satanic' influences exist. Keep in mind the polarization parameters and belief systems that are being upheld by egregores, or *collective thought forms,* in the matrix.

If the angel and devil are on either shoulder, one must reference neither and refer to Source, GOD, or the First Eye.

Once attuned to the Inner Sight, one can successfully raise the thought frequency above the trapping polarity parameters and redirect energy patterns accordingly to further protect Prana and harness Creative Life Force.

As we expand to Chapter Six, *Protecting Life Force,* the student will be given a brief note to assess, in order to raise their overall frequency and protect the *life essence* of their Being. This will be concise yet powerful as the male recognizes the VITAL importance of *controlling* their seed, and the female recognizes the VITAL importance as the mother and the womb; carrier of Life.

# CHAPTER SIX

## PROTECTING LIFE FORCE

This first portion of this chapter is in regards to the protection of sexual energies, reproductive organs, and sacred fluids of the individual. The demiurge, mentioned earlier, exists in the lower planes and traps energy in the lower aspects of the human Being. The demiurge assimilates *looping patterns*, usually consisting of all *weakening* forms of pleasure, gratification, and comfort, exhausting the spirit and altering vibrational frequencies of the individual to an unstable and imbalanced state, weakening electromagnetic fields, biological and neurological systems and their functioning.

This is a critical note for the reader, as one develops a *relationship with* their partner, and harmonious efforts are conducted for successful conception.

This is also assistive to the *relationship* one has with self, and raising awareness with Spirit to protect Prana from the lower possessive forces of lust, and refraining from engaging in non-meaningful sex, or vacuous relationships, or tending to parasitic organisms seeking your Life Force energy.

As for application, the first chapter, **Getting Closer to God,** details key codes for the material of the entire book. This is not deigned to be confusing, or to shift the student into another paradigm of thinking.

This is designed to empower the WILL of the Creative Process of the Individual, Awaken the Divine Life Spirit to further expansions across the Universe *inside* the mind and consciousness of the Alchemist. Your transmutability is your Creative Life Force and quite literally, *response-ability* within.

Every instance the individual discharges sexual and reproductive fluids without pure intention, life essence is negatively exhausted instead of preserved.

Continuously retrieving and depleting from the Potent Prana reservoir in the body leads to a stagnation, or *pattern loop,* blocking energy flow, specifically in the second Chakra center, the Sacral.

This is noted as a specific energy center for the individual who is making conscious efforts to heal and balance this area of themselves. In other words, developing healthier *relationships* with these lower energy centers in the student is VITAL. It is important to mention here, the key word *relationships.*

Notice that the student is **NOT** suggested to separate or remove themselves from *feelings* in the lower Chakra centers, including the gut, or (3) **Solar Plexus**, relating to will, personal power, self identification, metabolism, eating, self esteem, directly attached to the cerebrum by the vagus nerve and the enteric system (commonly called the 'second brain'), the (1) **Root** chakra at the base of the spine relating to control of vitality, stability, security, and as previously mentioned, the (2) **Sacral** Chakra, behind the belly button, relating to sexuality, pleasure, relationships, empathy and creativity.

The Soul journey consists of *balancing* all seven of these powerful faculties of human consciousness, through honorable creative expressions of action and Spirit (contemplation of self), requiring increasing efforts of the individual to willfully work with BOTH spiritual and material (animal) aspects of the Nature of their Being.

Additionally, resourcing the higher Intelligence Force to harness these faculties into the field of Creation through the electromagnetism of the heart, *equilibrium,* the most potent and powerful *toroidal* bio-field produced *by human consciousness*. Third, *utilizing* thought frequencies and *feeling* emotions (energy in motion) with intentions to keep the vibrational fields of the bio-electromagnetic currents healthy and balanced.

In efforts to keep the contents of this material in an easily digestible format, rather than repeating certain notes in greater detail, I, the author, humbly leave the true expansion process outside of the contents of these pages for YOU. After all, these are simply guide notes for the student to reference during the life endeavors one may be challenged by. The chapter pertaining to synchronistic awareness and pattern recognition will assist with detecting the synchronous universe from within, at thy will, enabling expansion of the Spirit and giving one agency of personal energy patterns inside the Matrix construct, Mother Earth.

# CHAPTER SEVEN

## PART ONE: THE MATERIAL PLANE

Nothing exists outside the Laws of the Universe in Gaia, the Matrix, as the Higher Order of Divine Intelligence operates as GOD and is *everything*. Generator, Operator, Destroyer. As the student develops awareness of the ability to harness and respond to higher consciousness, the more powerful the Creative Process in the life experience becomes; that is, to cultivate faculties of the imagination, Breath, Prana potential, innerstand and manifest Love in the highest forms of frequency. In exchange, the student willfully sacrifices indulgence in the lesser parts of the animalistic nature, in order to develop deeper Insight, wisdom, Intuition, Breath (Divine Life Force), and enhance overall well-being.

Polarization in the Material Plane has become well recognized to the student by this point in time, as well as previous methods which have been developed, and *innerstanding* has activated the non-dual connections of equal opposites inside of the polarity designs of the Matrix. This knowledge can be strategically applied to the Material Plane, for the Alchemist realizes the transmutability of thoughts and emotions have unlimited potential, and the ability to manifest anything must begin from the inner universe and flow into the creation field. The student has inner awareness of the Darkness, the subconscious mind, Blueprint of the Imagination, and the ability to willfully practice visualization. Harnessing emotions and *feeling* everything brings an extreme Intuitive Clarity to the individual. Innerstanding the power and *ability to respond* is within the *Chaos field* first, before it reaches the physical plane to manifest into the coded *Creation field*. The *chaos field IS* internal in the Mind of all human consciousness, and within the infinite Potential of the individual Mind is the harnessing power to bring *thought waveforms* from *Chaos into Creation through the equilibrium, or balance of the EM field of the **heart.***

Additionally, we have noted how to develop awareness and agency of synchronicities and pattern recognition, transmute energy patterns to higher fields of frequency for healing self, and helping other individuals *remember* they are capable of accomplishing *anything* in the faculties of the Mind. The student has acknowledged identification is shaped through mind, *not material.* Special abilities, equipment, or architecture are *not* required for an individual to convene with GOD. The cultivation of ALL *relationships* determine the human experience.

And you, traveler, have now become a Wolf, connected in the Deep Wilderness. Embrace this place. It is the most magical place for you to utilize and resource as endeavors persist in the life journey. This is now home, wherever one may BE, one possesses instant accessibility to traverse this magical universe and harness the Infinite Creative Potential that lies Within. One might have heard the phrase before, "home is where the *heart* is".......

The student is now fully embraced with ONE, with Prana, removed veils of polarity parameters, and innerstanding Spirit, the self-contemplative Life Force, and its perpetual emotions (energy in motion).

As a reminder, this material is compiled for the student to review ANYTIME along their adventure, and utilize at Will. There are not secrets, it has been said; everything is hidden in plain sight.

The student unravels the deeper meanings behind this message as one attunes to the inner universe and quiets the overstimulation and distractions of the external world.

With boundless potential to unlock, there is no need for I, the author, to keep your time wrapped up in 700 pages of background notes; this is more than enough to take a few grains and integrate what rings true and resonates with your Spirit. I truly intend this material to become a healthy *relationship pattern* with the reader, and never anything more or less. I have poured my Prana into this for you, and I hope you feel the Love and Power as you internalize the contents of **Peaks and Valleys.**

## *Additional Note from the Author*

*Dear readers, friends, family, supporters, and to whom this may concern:*

*From my **heart**, thank you so incredibly much for your love and support. I am inspired by each one of you who has interacted with me and contributed to my life experience. I am honored to present this material to you, and for these notes to be a small contributor and positive influence in your life experience. We are here to help each other remember we are part of One consciousness. If you will, share this with someone you Love. I will be presenting material as time permits me to do so. Thank you, again.*

*If you would like to contact me directly, please do not hesitate to reach out to me. This is not professional or medical advice from a doctor. I am simply just the alarm ringing to the Spirit to live its highest Purpose in human consciousness. With Love,*
*-JLS*

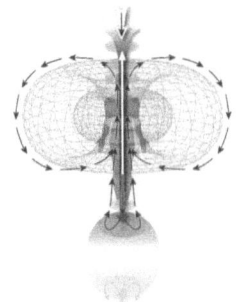

ISBN 978-1-966313-01-4

US$21.17

9 781966 313014

5 2 1 1 7 >

www.ingramcontent.com/pod-product-compliance
Lightning Source LLC
Chambersburg PA
CBHW030517130626
46549CB00007B/3036